CW00386078

Fox Talbot

THE NATIONAL TRUST

Fox Talbot's calotype camera made by Chevalier of Paris *c.*1845. Royal Photographic Society Collection.

William Henry Fox Talbot was born at Melbury in Dorset on 11 February 1800, at the home of the Earl of Ilchester; his mother, Lady Elizabeth Fox-Strangways, was the eldest daughter of the Earl. His father, William Davenport Talbot, an army officer, died when Henry was only six months old so Lady Elisabeth and her son spent the early years of his life in the homes of various relatives.

A brilliant child and gifted scholar, he excelled, both at Harrow and Cambridge, in the classics and sciences.

In 1827 he returned to his ancestral home, Lacock Abbey, where he was Lord of the Manor. In 1832 he married Constance Mundy of Markeaton Hall in Derbyshire. In 1831 he became MP for Chippenham, but only remained in Parliament for about two years.

His interests then took him abroad, particularly to Italy. On his travels he used a camera lucida and a camera obscura, optical aids to drawing, which gave him the idea of retaining permanently the images these aids produced.

From 1850 Fox Talbot concentrated on perfecting reproduction techniques, so that original photographs could be reproduced as printed illustrations. He coated metal plates with bichromated gelatine using silk to form a screen pattern, patenting this process in 1852.

The span of Fox Talbot's life embraces an age of tremendous progress in the arts and sciences in Britain and Europe. When he died in September 1877, he was one of the rare people who had made significant contributions to the advances in both these fields.

Lacock Abbey from the River Avon. Calotype by William Henry Fox Talbot. Lacock Abbey Collection.

William Henry Fox Talbot. Portrait by Moffatt of Edinburgh, 1864.

Fox Talbot was a classicist as well as a scientist and contributed to many published papers and scientific works.

His two volumes on Classical and Antiquarian Researches, published by Longmans in 1838 put forward some new arguments, while his solutions to obtuse mathematical problems led to his election as a Fellow of the Royal Society in 1831. In 1838 he was awarded the Society's Royal Medal for his researches on the integral calculus, and in 1842 gained the Rumford Medal for his photographic discoveries.

In the 1850s, Fox Talbot began work on the Assyrian script, an interest which was to last the rest of his life. He became so expert in translating this complex cuneiform writing that he was asked to contribute as an Examiner for the British Museum. He also gave financial support to archaeological expeditions.

Fox Talbot never went to Egypt, but might have been given these tablets, or bought them, c.1856. Lacock Abbey Collection.

Some of the classical researches published privately by Fox Talbot, together with middle period Egyptian tablets, arranged in the South Gallery, Lacock Abbey.

Fox Talbot went to Harrow School in 1811. He joined the house of Dr George Butler, a brilliant scholar who encouraged the young Fox Talbot's interest in the sciences.

He studied at Trinity College, Cambridge, between 1819 and 1821, becoming 12th Wrangler in Mathematics in 1821.

Coming down from Cambridge, he spent some time travelling in Europe, where he met distinguished European scientists. In the 1830s, he turned his mind to problems of optics, magnetic experiments, and the study of perception of vision. The machine he used for this latter experiment is on view in the Museum.

Fox Talbot's spark generating apparatus.
At Harrow School, when he was 11, he carried out a series of experiments often leading to explosions. Between 1840 and 1852 he took out four patents involving mechanisms using electricity as a motive power, i.e. converting electrical energy into mechanical energy.

Fox Talbot was fascinated by the optical sciences. The illustration shows the wooden apparatus made for him to study the phenomenon of perception of vision.

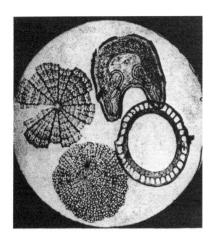

A study of Fox Talbot's surviving notebooks reveals the breadth of his scientific researches, which encompassed astronomy, spectrography, microscopy – he was the first scientist to use the polarizing microscope.

Two prints from his experiments in photomicroscopy using a solar microscope (see illustration) are in the Lacock Abbey Collection and are illustrations of a lantern fly's wing and a section of three plant stems.

Fox Talbot's work on the analysis of minerals through flame, using the spectrometer was an advance. He was also interested in electricity and the use of vacuum pumps. Examples of these machines are on view in the Museum.

Two examples of the early photomicrographs: three plant sections and that of a lantern fly's wing taken by Fox Talbot using his solar microscope *c.*1839.

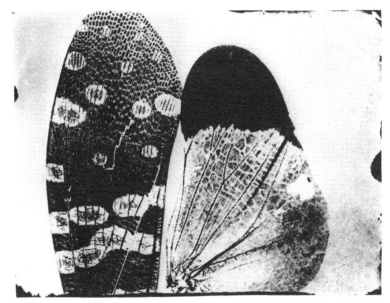

A solar microscope. This apparatus was placed in a window where the sun's rays were deflected from a mirror through the microscope facing a darkened room. The specimen on the slide was then projected on a wall. This solar microscope is from the Cyril Permutt Collection.

Fox Talbot's polarising microscope. His work on microscopy using polarised light contributed to research in this field in the 1820s and 1830s. Lacock Abbey Collection.

Fox Talbot's vacuum pump. This was possibly used in his experiments with minerals and gases.

Fox Talbot used a camera lucida, an optical aid to drawing, to record sketches of the reflected scene by Lake Como in 1834.

He wondered how he could retain the lovely scene permanently and this was the idea which led him to his first efforts in what is now known as photography.

By coating drawing paper with salt solution and then, after it had dried, adding a solution of silver nitrate, and placing a leaf, or piece of lace, on the paper's surface in a press and exposing it to the sun, he obtained an image which he called a photogenic drawing. These were paper negatives from which positives could be made. Fixing was achieved in solutions of salt.

Prompted by the work on photography by the Frenchman, Louis Daguerre, Fox Talbot announced his own findings in a paper read to a meeting at the Royal Society on 31 January 1839. He called his paper 'Account of the Art of Photogenic Drawing or the process by which natural objects may be made to delineate themselves without the aid of the artist's pencil'.

Photogenic drawing of a leaf *c*.1835–40.

Below: Another original wooden printing frame used by Fox Talbot. Lacock Abbey Collection.

A fern leaf was often used as a subject by Fox Talbot in his early photographic experiments with solutions of salt and silver nitrate. He called these prints 'photogenic drawings'. The illustration shows Fox Talbot's original printing frame with Lacock Abbey in the background.

Fox Talbot used different patterns of lace as subjects for his photogenic drawings, particularly these creative shadow patterns which he made up to the mid 1840s, after his later calotype process had been patented.

The exposure times using a camera obscura were in the region of an hour or two although photographic images of the abbey were produced within that time.

Fox Talbot realised that by reducing the size of the wooden box and using lenses of shorter focal lengths the exposure time would also be reduced.

His earliest small cameras were probably made by the local village carpenter, and some still survive in the collections of the Science Museum and the Royal Photographic Society. One of these has been loaned to the Museum (see illustration).

The negative taken by Fox Talbot of the oriel window at Lacock Abbey also still exists and is in the Science Museum collection (see illustration).

Latticed Window
(with the Camera Obscura)
August 1835

When first made, the squares of glass about 200 in number could be counted, with help of a lens.

Fox Talbot's original camera, affectionately called by his mother 'Henry's little mousetrap', photographed in the lattice window in the South Gallery, Lacock Abbey. This window is the subject of the world's earliest authenticated surviving negative, and is only $1\frac{3}{8}$ by $1\frac{1}{8}$ inches in size.

From 1839 Fox Talbot bought his cameras from Ross of London, the instrument and lens maker, and also from Chevalier in Paris.

With the improvement in lens manufacture, the photographic images were sharper and the exposure times much shorter.

By 1840 Fox Talbot had improved his photographic researches using gallic acid to increase the sensitivity of the bromine paper, and by October 1839 had developed what today would be the 'latent image'.

He took many pictures with cameras ranging in size from $3 \times 3\frac{1}{2}$ in. up to $8\frac{1}{2} \times 6\frac{1}{2}$ in. and he named the process 'Calotype', a word derived from the Greek '*kalos*', meaning beautiful.

One great advantage of this improved process was that, with exposures of minutes or less, portraits could be taken and some of the earliest pictures in 1840 were of his family.

At this time he took his famous calotype photographs using a ladder as the focal point in the composition.

The Haystack and the Ladder are typical examples of his creative work.

The Ladder, an important subject which Fox Talbot chose for Plate XIV of *The Pencil of Nature*.

Fox Talbot's portrait camera purchased from Ross of London who supplied most of his cameras. Royal Photographic Society Collection.

The Haystack, selected for Plate X in Fox Talbot's famous publication *The Pencil of Nature*. In describing this picture he observed: 'One discovery of the Photographic Art will be, that it will enable us to introduce in our pictures a multitude of minute details which add to the truth and reliability of the representation.'

In a letter to Lord Landsdown, Fox Talbot calculated it had cost him £5,000 to bring his photographic invention to perfection. This was a considerable sum and Fox Talbot thought about recovering some of the cost by setting up a printing works. No 55 Russell Terrace, now called Baker Street, Reading was in operation from 1844 to 1846.

The most important publication produced at Reading was Fox Talbot's *Pencil of Nature*, a six-part series describing his invention of photography with an artistic appreciation of the 24 prints tipped into the accompanying text. This is the first publication produced for sale which has photographic illustrations.

The business however was not a great commercial success, and by early 1847 Fox Talbot decided to close it down. But there is no doubt that despite this failure, William Henry Fox Talbot can rightly be called 'The Father of Modern Photography'.

Below: Two original calotypes formed together to show a view of the Reading Establishment. The man in the centre is thought to be Fox Talbot himself.

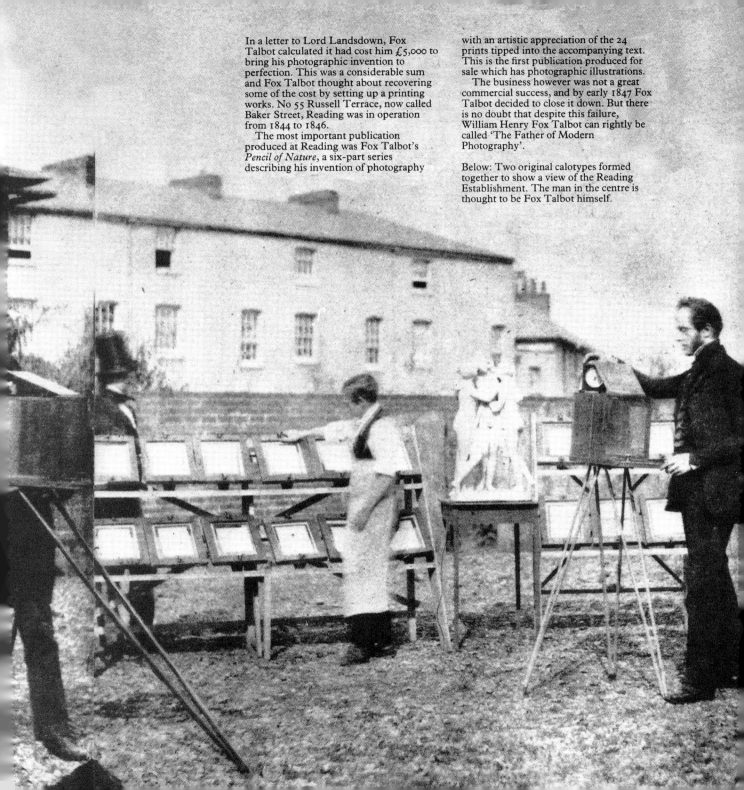

Fox Talbot, although the inventor of the negative/positive process of photography, rarely allowed himself to be photographed. In 1866 or 1867, however, the family posed in the Lacock Abbey Cloisters for the photographer J M Bloomfield of Hastings. The picture shows (left to right) Charles Henry his son, W H F Talbot, his daughter Ela; seated: Rosamond his daughter and Constance, Mrs Fox Talbot. A third daughter, Matilda, was not living at the Abbey at the time having married a Mr Gilchrist-Clerk of Dumfries, Scotland.

Portrait of Antoine Claudet, a colleague of Fox Talbot. He became a well-known portrait photographer using the daguerreotype process, although he also used Talbot's calotype system.

Three estate workers at Lacock Abbey.
In order to ensure stillness for the necessary two minutes,
the group is posed holding on to various chairs.

Portrait by Fox Talbot of Claudet (right)
playing chess with a friend, taken in
Claudet's London studio.

On his visits to London, Fox Talbot stayed in Sackville Street in the house of his step-father, Captain Feilding RN. During these visits he photographed a number of London scenes, including his club, the Athenaeum, the Hungerford Suspension Bridge designed by Brunel in 1845, and the Royal Naval Hospital, Greenwich. One of the most interesting was his photograph of Nelson's Column nearing completion late in 1843, before the siting of the lions by Landseer which were added in 1845.

Fox Talbot's interest in engineering, and especially Brunel's inventions in the railways and shipping, resulted in a rare calotype of the SS *Great Britain* taken at Bristol in 1846 before her first voyage.

Fox Talbot travelled often to Europe, taking his camera with him to France and Belgium. The collection at Lacock Abbey has a number of the photographs from his travels. The picture of the boulevard in Paris was taken from a window in his hotel in 1843.

Construction of Nelson's Column, Trafalgar Square, photographed by Fox Talbot in 1843.

The photographs by Fox Talbot in this booklet are the first examples of the art of photography. Study of these and others in the Lacock Abbey Collection reveals a creative imagery in composition which reflects Fox Talbot's approach to his subjects.

His scientific and classical knowledge, a rare combination, his study of languages, archaeology, his concern for the derivation of words and his feeling for painting all contributed to the way he arranged objects in relation to subjects and space to produce photographic images of unique quality.

He realised, too, his invention was the beginning of visual communication for he says in *The Pencil of Nature*: 'The chief object of the present work is to place on record some of the beginning of a new art, before the period, which we must be approaching, of its being brought to maturity by the aid of British talent'.

Calotype by Fox Talbot of an elm tree on the Lacock Abbey estate.
Fox Talbot was interested in botany and was
a great plantsman all his life.

Calotype of an oak probably in Carclew Park, Cornwall, the home of Sir Charles Lemon, brother-in-law of Fox Talbot's mother, Lady Elisabeth Fox-Strangways.

The Fruit piece, still-life calotype by Fox Talbot
which he used as one of the illustrations in the *Pencil of Nature*.

Portrait of Mrs Fox Talbot in ermine cape,
and her three daughters, Ela, Rosamond
and Matilda (Science Museum Collection).

Portrait of Fox Talbot's youngest daughter
Matilda, *c.*1844.

On the subject of portraiture Fox Talbot
observed: 'When a person has been
artistically arranged, and trained by a little
practice to maintain an absolute
immobility for a few seconds, very
delightful pictures are easily obtained.'

Calotype portrait of an unknown man,
probably a guest at the Abbey, *c.*1845.

In *The Pencil of Nature* Fox Talbot
describes the taking of portraits: 'Portraits
of living persons form one of the most
attractive subjects of photography but we
cannot well succeed in this branch of the art
without some previous concert and
arrangement.'

Portrait of a lady in a striped dress, possibly a member of the
Lacock Abbey household.

Fox Talbot understood the importance of the interest and
reality of photographic portraiture, writing 'What would not
be the value to our English nobility of such a record of their
ancestors who lived a century ago!'

River bridge at Malines, a calotype photograph taken by Fox Talbot in 1846.

Fox Talbot made a number of lengthy
journeys in Europe, taking his camera and
accessories with him. He went to Brussels in
October 1846 and visited Malines (now
called Mechelen), where he took this view in
the cathedral town.